Essential Christian Leadership

Chris Palmer

Christian Leadership by Chris Palmer

First Published in Great Britain in 2019. Printed and bound in Great Britain by Marston Book Services Limited, Oxfordshire.

FAITHBUILDERS An Imprint of Apostolos Publishing Ltd, 3rd Floor, 207 Regent Street, London W1B 3HH

www.apostolos-publishing.com

British Library Cataloguing-in-Publication Data. A catalogue record for this book is available from the British Library

ISBN: 978-1-912120-32-1

Cover Design by Faithbuilders. Cover Image © Tuk69tuk | Dreamstime.com

Essentials of Christian Leadership

Chris Palmer

Contents

Preface by the Author

The Essentials of Christian Leadership is a result of serving and leading in local church and para-church organisations. This short introductory book has been adapted from a series of lectures delivered as part of the MTh degree programme at a Bible Seminary in SE. Asia. My thanks to the students who helped me shape the thinking in a cross-cultural setting which challenged many of my preconceived westernised views of the Bible and leadership. It is my hope and prayer that this short book will help you as you contemplate or engage in Christian leadership in the 21st century.

My thanks also to Mathew Bartlett at Apostolos Christian Publishing, for his help in editing and suggesting a few alterations to make the text more acceptable for publication.

Finally, thanks to Jayne and Tom who allow me to study and travel to facilitate training in the UK and further afield; where would I be without your support!

Chris Palmer

March 2019

Essentials of Christian Leadership

> Shepherd the flock of God that is among you, exercising oversight, not under compulsion but willingly, as God would have you. 1 Pet 5:2

Leadership is a vital element in the life of the local church, and although it is often overlooked, it is a subject that requires serious attention. Sometimes leadership is left to those who volunteer because no one else 'will step up to the plate'. Sadly, even though they may be willing to help such individuals can be ineffective if they are not called by God to the ministry, which is the first and most important qualification for the serious task of leading God's people.

The biblical narrative focusses on many leaders and records the 'good the bad and the indifferent'. All of these provide us with examples, whether good or bad, from which we can learn. This book does not set out to examine every biblical leader – that would be a book too large to handle! However, it does provide an overview of leadership from a biblical perspective and sets out ten principles that will help leaders and prospective leaders. These principles have been developed over time as I have led and been led within the context of local church and para-church organisations. It is not a guaranteed manual of success but a helpful guide to the study and practice of this essential ministry. I trust that as you read these pages you will be helped, encouraged and challenged. More than anything, I pray that you may enjoy some success in your leadership as you adopt the Essentials of Christian Leadership.

Sometimes, it is a matter of coping with each situation as it comes. Leadership is challenging in many ways and all Christian leaders need to stand firm on Christ his calling and revelation. Sometimes the task may seem dark however, leaders must never forget what God has called them to in the light and never doubt their divine calling to lead his people.

Leadership studies often focus attention on the leader: who you are in God and what God desires of you so that you can be that positive, spiritual influence upon those you lead. Such influence is only achievable as you walk close to the Lord and observe all the spiritual disciplines in a regular and systematic manner. However, any leadership study must also focus on the God who calls us to leadership and the people whom we are called to lead. True biblical spiritual leadership arises from a heart focussed on the love of God, which is demonstrated in loving the people of God.

Before you proceed to read this book stop and consider the following questions:

- Where are you in your relationship to God?
- Where are you in your relationship to the people of God?

Until or unless you first commit yourself wholly to God and the service of his people then you cannot be a proficient leader in the church of God. In fact, if God is not first in your life and experience then as you 'lead' you will do more harm than good, and you will hurt more than you help. Set out to put God first!

The Christian shepherd who leads God's flock must first be led by the Lord, who is "my Shepherd" (Ps 23), the good and great shepherd (John 10:11; Heb 13:20).

Chris Palmer

Ten Essentials of Christian Leadership

1. Character.
2. Clear vision.
3. Commitment.
4. Servanthood.
5. Compassion.
6. Courage.
7. Communication.
8. Complementarity.
9. Confidentiality.
10. Leading by Love.

Each of these essential principles will be dealt with in its own chapter. It is my hope and prayer that as this book is read it will impact lives on a spiritual level and help leaders refocus their attention on the spiritual nature of their God-given task.

Biblical Leadership

In the Christian church, the role of the leader should never be confused with the role of a manger. In the Bible, Christian leaders are instead compared to shepherds, who are chosen by God to lead, protect and help the people of God to grow. What the 21st century church requires are shepherd-leaders who are focussed on God, committed to his will and purposes, with a heart for people and a desire to see the gospel impact communities in a powerful way.

Where are these people? This is a question that I have pondered for many years and am becoming increasingly concerned about the lack of biblical leaders. What can we do? Pray in response to the words of Jesus in Matt 9:38; 'Therefore pray earnestly to the Lord of the harvest to send out labourers into his harvest.'

Let's seek God to produce people who will stand for the gospel, not compromising the truth and not set on pleasing every ideology. People with God in their heart and God at the heart of everything, with a desire to serve. If leaders are willing to stand up and honor God, he has assured us that he will honour us:

> If anyone serves me, he must follow me; and where I am, there will my servant be also. If anyone serves me, the Father will honour him. John 12:26.

This verse contains some important principles: i) service is necessary; ii) following Jesus is necessary to successful service; iii) remaining close to Jesus is vital for the true servant; iv) the honour of God will be experienced, that is, God values his servants as such he guarantees his presence on earth and recompense for diligence in eternal glory. This should motivate those who lead to understand leadership as service of God who is the rewarder of those who follow him and stand for the truth.

Are you willing to take the stand for the truth of the gospel and grow closer to Jesus? Will you commit to know God seeking his rewards and not be taken up with earthly honour? Too many leaders are seeking to please their fellow humanity and receive plaudits for their work than are set on seeking God even if this means putting the world's standards and selfish desires to one side.

Leaders, it's time to get serious with God about the great task of leading God's people through this life in a manner that brings glory to God and impacts lives for eternity.

What are we leading?

Leadership too often focusses on the individual without giving due consideration to the people whom we are called to lead and serve. It is imperative that we understand the who and what of leadership. The church is the focus of biblical leadership and in order to get a fuller picture of leadership we must first have a better understanding of the church. John Stott writes:

> We urgently need a healthy, biblical understanding of the church, for only then shall we have a healthy, biblical understanding of Christian leadership. We must not define the church in terms of its leaders but rather define leaders in relation to the church.[1]

Stott's comment provokes us to think about how we structure leadership in our churches. Do we begin with a leader/person and fit them in to the church or do we

---

[1] John Stott, *Basic Christian Leadership*, (Downers Grove, IL: IVP, 2002) 93.

begin with the church and discover the type of leaders it requires? I believe that if we adopt this second approach, this could cause a fundamental shift in the search for leaders in the local church. What does your church require for it to grow in God? This question should be one we ask every time there is a pastor, elder, deacon or council member chosen to serve. The focus must be the church, not the leader; the people, not the 'figure head'; the flock, not the shepherd; and God's will, not man's ideas. It is important that we do not simply endeavour to replicate a previous leader when choosing a new one. Every leader is there for a 'season' and as the seasons of nature change so too leadership seasons change. There is generally a need for a change of leader as this will allow for a fresh perspective on church life and practice. Don't be afraid of change and don't think that the next leader must be a clone of the previous one however good their leadership. Be sure it is God's person for the season and a person who has the heart for God and his people.

The church is a living body inaugurated by Jesus Christ, and it exists for the benefit of the wider community and not simply the church members. Hence, we must be very careful that we are not producing a church that caters solely for the membership but remember the importance of the church's mission to non-members.

The church could be summarised as follows:

1. A called-out group (2 Cor 6:16–18).

2. A living organism (1 Pet 2:5).
3. The means of enabling discipleship (Eph 2:19–22; 4:12–13).
4. The means of disseminating the gospel (Eph 3:8–10).

Here, we must recognise that the church is about people not places, it's about needs not structures and it is about God's desires and not human wishes. If we can reassess what we think of as 'the church' and move away from a building filled with people singing and worshipping, we will come closer to the New Testament ideal. I submit that the 21st century church needs to be a 'missional' body reaching out through every member. Each member needs to be properly equipped for service (Eph 4:11–12). This is where the importance of biblical leadership is essential; for it is the leaders who are equipped to equip. Leadership then places the emphasis upon people to redefine the nature and purpose of the church and to focus on how we deal with people, problems and possibilities and discover solutions to situations faced by the ordinary 'man in the street'.

Traditions: The good, the bad & the unnecessary

A major issue faced by churches and leaders is that of tradition. As R. L. Sturch writes:

Any group that lasts for a long time develops traditions: customs, beliefs or habits of thought, some of which are deliberately passed down and some of which are taken largely for granted.[2]

The menace of tradition haunts most leaders throughout their tenure at churches around the world; they can be a blessing or a curse! It is vital to establish the difference between the good, the bad and the unnecessary. While some people are reluctant to exchange tradition for the biblical position, progress will only come as God's word is put before human tradition. As you consider the church and its traditions contemplate this question

Why do we do what we do?

Your answer to this will prove essential in deciding what is good, bad or unnecessary. As a leader it will fall to you to differentiate between the various traditions and to have the courage to rid the church of the bad and unnecessary and emphasise the good.

Take a few moments to think through the things that you do at church. Then apply the question, why do we do that? Now consider if it is necessary to act and deal biblically and sympathetically with some of those traditions and endeavour to move the church forward and away from the unnecessary. This may be painful for some and will result in open criticism and hostility

---

[2] R.L. Sturch, *IVP Dictionary of Christian Ethics*, (Leicester: IVP, 1995), 858.

from others but if it's God's will then stick to your principles and trust God for the grace to carry through his plan.

As we discuss the nature and purpose of the church, we must consider Paul's words in 1 Tim 3:15, the church is:

> the household of God, which is the church of the living God, the pillar and support of truth.

The church and its leaders are here for a purpose; some points to remember from this verse:

1. The church is God's not ours! (Matt 16:18).
2. The church is a living entity (1 Pet 2:4–5).
3. The church is a support for the truth (1 Cor 3:11).
4. The church provides a firm foundation (Eph 2:19–22).
5. The church is the place of truth (2 Tim 2:15).

Is the church you are part of following this divine pattern in its operation and practices? The relation of the church to the truth is important as it introduces the subject of absolutes. The Bible, the truth, must be the basis for all church praxis. As a Christian leader it will be your responsibility to ensure that the Bible is the basis for all church life. This will obviously be dictated to by your view of the Bible; it is the absolute truth which is to be used as the basis for faith and practice.

Worship

A major aspect of the church is worship; this is a whole life issue (Rom 12:1) and not simply 20–40 minutes of singing or noise! This should be seen in all aspects of church life and could be summarised as follows:

1. Gathering (Acts 1:6).
2. Prayer (Acts 1:14).
3. Preaching (Acts 1:2–4).
4. Breaking Bread (Acts 2:42).
5. Singing (Eph 5:9).
6. Spiritual gifts (Rom 12:6).
7. Reading Bible (1 Tim 4:13).
8. Tithing (1 Cor 16:1–2).
9. Sharing (Acts 2:45).
10. Edification (1 Cor 14:26).
11. Evangelism (Matt 9:37–38).

All these elements make up the worship of the church and as leaders it is imperative that these elements are promoted and maintain through your ministry and service. Modelling a life of worship and service is a key element of leadership; people will only respond to your ministry if they see you living as a sacrifice to Jesus.

The purpose of the church could be summarised in the following 6 points which should also relate to its leaders:

1. Preach the gospel (2 Tim 4:5).
2. Preach the word (Titus 1:9).
3. Disciple converts (2 Tim 2:2).

4. Pray for the community (1 Tim 2:1–8).
5. Help the needy (Jas 1:27).
6. Set an example (1 Cor 13).

If this is the basis of the purpose of your local church, then I suggest you are on the right path to serving as God intended. If these elements are missing from your local church, then it may be time to reassess where you are and what you are doing for the sake of the gospel. It is good practice to set out the 'Core Values' of the church you lead, engage the leadership team in a discussion of these values, and draw up 5 or 6 points that focus the purpose of the church. Then once these have been agreed share them with the church, minster on them explain them to the congregation and keep them visible as a reminder of why the church exists. Adopting a corporate identity which pervades every ministry of the church producing a 'holistic' approach to church ministry will prove tough but is worthwhile in uniting the church behind the vision.

Why does the church require leadership?

A question that must be answered. Why can't we simply leave things to happen and trust the Holy Spirit to have complete control? It's because if we do chaos could break out and the church becomes a free-for-all and not a pillar of the truth. Hence, the church requires leadership because of people's propensity to argue, disagree and generally want their own way! The problem that can occur is seen in the Book of Judges, where the phrase used to describe the people of God was, 'everyone did what was right in his own eyes' (Judg 17:6). This was purely because there was no strong leadership guiding the people in the ways of God. The same can happen in the local church. Where there is no recognised biblical, God ordained leadership people will do their own thing resulting in chaos and ineffective ministry.

Why leadership? The biblical paradigm suggests the following reasons:

1. Christ the head is our example (Eph 1:22–23).
2. Leaders set spiritual example (1 Pet 5:3).
3. Leadership provides accountability (Acts 13:1–3).
4. Provides care for the congregation (1 Pet 5:1–3).
5. Equips disciples (Eph 4:11–12).
6. Makes decisions (Acts 15).
7. Ensures against false teaching (Acts 20).
8. Teaches the congregation (Acts 6:4).
9. Shares the load (Acts 6:1–7).
10. Settles disputes (Acts 15).

Strong biblical leadership is required on a local level to ensure the wholesomeness of the local church is maintained. This will then promote spiritual growth and impact the wider community. Leaders are necessary to guide, direct, correct, equip and facilitate the purposes of God through the local congregation. Leadership matters!

Who should lead?

John Stott writes:

> A leader, according to its simplest definition, is someone who commands a following. To lead is to go ahead, to show the way and to inspire other people to follow.[3]

Leaders are necessary wherever there is a group of people. All groups require a focus and that is invariably the one recognised as the leader. There have been many great leaders throughout history both in the biblical narrative and general world history; a general principle that links them all is that they commanded a following. Great leaders, whether good or bad, had a major impact upon their societal context because they were committed to their cause and willing to promote it at any cost. It doesn't matter if you are a statesman or a religious figure commitment to your cause is essential. Harry S. Truman wrote:

> A leader is a person who has the ability to get others to do what they don't want to, and like it.[4]

'Leader' is not a word widely used in the biblical narrative (1 Chron 12:27; 13:1; 2 Chron 32:21; Isa 9:46; 55:4; Matt 15:14).

---

[3] John Stott, *Calling Christian Leaders*, (Leicester: IVP, 2002), 9.

[4] J. Oswald Saunders, *Spiritual Leadership*, (Chicago: Moody, 1994), 28.

In these references, it is interesting to note the people in question are generally military leaders and not spiritual figures. However, the Bible promotes 'shepherds' as the major paradigm for spiritual leadership and although people are called to lead, they are not referred to as leaders but servants and shepherds. (Josh 1:1; Mark 10:42–45; John 12:26; Rom 1:1; Jas 1:1; 2 Pet 1:1; Jude 1:1).

The heart of the shepherd is revealed in Ps 23 where the care, provision, support, correction and love of the shepherd are recorded. It is worthwhile to assess your life and leadership skills in respect to the Ps 23 paradigm; do you follow the good shepherd's example as you lead the flock of God?

Called by God

I'm sorry to say that simply reading this book will not make you a leader in God's church, for only God can call and equip you for this task. A true Christian leader is one who has been chosen by God and called to serve John 15:15–17 refers to the revolutionary nature of the teaching of Jesus. He chose us to follow him and not as was the norm in his day that a disciple chose a Rabbi to follow. Again, Jesus is turning our natural perspective on its head and placing himself at the centre of all we are and do.

Are you called by God to serve through leading?

Recognising the call of God

Becoming a leader is a serious matter that should never be entered lightly; all leaders must know the call of God. How is this call recognised?

1. The inner call (Is 30:21) is a sense of inner compulsion, desire or witness in one's spirit which manifests itself in an all absorbing desire to lead God's people. In this situation the individual knows a sense of leading, purpose and growing commitment to that ministry.

2. The external call (Phil 2:19–23) is when a congregation recognises in an individual the qualities of godly leadership and requests their help in leading. Such people evaluate and affirm the call placed on an individual.

3. Confirmation through the word of God (Is 30:21) may come to you as you read a passage or hearing a message that confirms your inner call.

4. Love for the people of God (Eph 4:11–14). No leader will be successful unless they possess a deep love for God's people and their spiritual well-being. All leaders are there to build people up in spiritual matters this is a result of love working through them.

5. Obedience to the voice of God (1 Sam 3:9; Is 6:8). There is nothing sadder than a person who rejects the voice of God and ignores God's promptings to leadership. The individual who

is called to lead must be open, listening and responsive to the voice of God.

As you consider your calling to leadership, remember that it is a divine calling, not a career. Leadership is not a job to be done but a vocation to fulfil. It is a mission given to us by God not a nice idea from self or others.

When one progresses into leadership there are two issues to be aware of:

1.   The leader is a spiritual person, the natural must not dominate their life. The Holy Spirit must have control over heart, mind and spirit (1 Cor 6:19–20; 9:27; 2 Cor 5:14; 1 Tim 3).
2.   The leader must glorify God in all they do and never use their position to promote self or any other person (Acts 2:36; 1 Cor 1:23; 2:1–2; 3:11).

The leader must put aside all personal agendas, prejudices, desires and thoughts and focus on God and his people. They must be people who have a desire to see the kingdom of God extended and established in the lives of others. D. E. Hoste of the China Inland Mission gives an excellent benchmark to assess leaders:

It occurs to me that perhaps the best test of whether one is qualified to lead, is to find out whether anyone is following.[5]

---

[5] Sanders, *Spiritual Leadership*, 28.

Are people following you? Or are you causing people to flounder in their faith? Consider your calling!

Once called it is necessary for the individual to adopt a correct strategy for leadership. I suggest the following: B.U.I.L.D.

Build on solid foundations (Eph 2:20).

Utilise knowledge (1 Cor 11:1).

Identify needs; what is really needed in this situation?

Locate answers/limit damage – bring a biblical solution.

Develop a strategy which will bring success to the situation.

All of these require the leader to be focussed on God and God's ways of moving his people forward. Are you ready to BUILD for the glory of God and not simply to promote self or receive accolades from others?

Moses, the reluctant leader: a case study.

Moses provides some helpful insights into the way in which God calls and equips people for leadership. Moses had one of the most difficult roles ever given to anyone and was reluctant to take the reins. However, he succeeded in God's strength. Read through Exodus and examine the leadership issues Moses faced:

1. Reluctance (Exod 3:11).
2. Humility (Exod 3:13–16).
3. Divine empowering (Exod 4:1–9).
4. Recognition of weakness (Exod 4:10–13).
5. Followed God's lead (Exod 13:17–22).
6. Faith (Exod 14:13–31).
7. Dealing with disputes (Exod 18:13–16).
8. Willingness to learn (Exod 18:17–27).
9. Delivers the word of God (Exod 20–31).
10. Defends against false worship (Exod 32).
11. Intercedes for the people of God (Exod 33:12–23).
12. Fulfilled the commands of God (Exod 40).

You may feel a little or lot like Moses, inadequate to take the lead however, if God has called then he will equip, guide and complete the work in you which is necessary for those you are leading. Leadership may frighten you, it may worry you but if God has called you, go with that calling and fulfil your potential to lead God's people. Perhaps, just as with Moses, there is a 'promised land' of blessing ahead for your church, congregation or organisation.

In this book, I suggest 10 essential principles for Christian leadership. These serve as a general introduction to the qualities and characteristics required from a biblical Christian leader. I hope they will help as you contemplate this serious subject.

Chapter 1: Character

> For he was a good man full of the Holy Spirit and of faith. Acts 11:24.

This pen sketch of Barnabas introduces the first essential element of Christian leadership: a good character. Barnabas supported and led the early church and obtained an excellent testimony; all leaders should seek to emulate the example of Barnabas.

The character of an individual is a combination of their attributes, experiences, disposition, reputation, qualities and temperament that distinguishes them from others. God wants to produce in all his people a good character (Rom 5:4), and building a godly character is something we can all work on. The goal of all true Christian character is to be more Christ like. Is the desire to be like Jesus your driving principle? If it is you are on the right road to developing the true character of a Christian leader.

A leader's character may be tested when they are on their own, in a tight spot or under attack. Who and what you are in public must match who you are in private? One's inner self dictates who you are, what you do and how you do it. The private life of the leader must mirror his/her public persona. Don't let yourself down by acting out leadership and abusing your position in private.

A Christian leader's character should be characterised by spiritual reliability, trustworthiness, honesty, integrity, steadfastness, calmness, thoughtfulness and helpfulness. This is possible as the leader places their personal development in the hands of God. A strong character is also necessary as there will be times of loneliness, disappointment, opposition and doubt; all will need to be met head-on and strength of character will see the leader through.

To assess your character, it's a good exercise to sit and write down your strengths and weaknesses. As you consider them it will help you ascertain where you are in terms of character development. If you struggle with this exercise, consider the following:

1. Who are you when you are on your own?
2. What do you think about?
3. Who are you when things are difficult?
4. How do you react to criticism?
5. How do you react to praise?
6. Do you work well alone?
7. Do you work well in a team?
8. Do you have a sense of humour?
9. Are you emotionally aware?
10. What is your priority in life?

The development of one's character is affected by many and varied forces. A frequently overlooked aspect of our character is ancestry, whereby one inherits certain qualities or traits. Add to this the experiences of childhood and youth, which can have a significant effect upon the developing character. The influences we face can be many and varied, and how one assimilates those experiences will affect one's character. Coupled with this is the influence of one's social environment. Difficult financial and social conditions will impact the development of our characters in a different way to that of someone who has been brought up in comfort and ease. Exposure to education, work environment, media, associates and friends will also influence character development. However, there is still that important aspect of how one allows those varied influences to affect one's development.

> Character is not created in isolation or repose; it's forged through interaction with others and the world.[6]

We are not islands and are affected by so many different forces that we cannot develop in isolation. That's what Paul was aiming at in Rom 5:3–5, where he lists the external influences that can lead to a 'proven character' (NASB); 'tested character' (Douglas Moo) or 'well-formed character' (N.T. Wright)[7]. That is the character of a person who is proved or approved by God and others. Biblically it is interesting to notice how

---

[6] David Corbett, *99 Essential Quotes on Character*, www.writingeekery.com

[7] Douglas Moo, *The Epistle to Romans* (Grand Rapids: Eerdmans, 1996); N. T. Wright, *Romans for Everyone* (London: SPCK, 2004).

testing or tribulations produces a well-rounded character. John Maxwell writes:

> Crisis doesn't necessarily make character, but it certainly does reveal it.[8]

Maxwell perhaps doesn't go as far as I do by suggesting that crisis develops individual character, but his sentiments are correct. The true character of leadership is often best seen when under fire!

Romans 5:4 and the development of a 'proven character' follows the idea of testing metals in the fire to prove them or strengthen them to make them useful (see also Zech 13:9). This theme is developed in the New Testament by Peter (1 Pet 1:6–9 and 2 Pet 1:5–8). The development of a useful character focuses on purifying the individual from within but often through outward sources and situations. This pure character is a series of qualities upon which one should build thereby making the individual a godly example to others – how important this is in leadership. As you read the verses in 2 Pet 1:5–8 ask yourself, 'How am I doing in developing these character traits'? Consider their importance to you and adopt a policy to seek them and add them to your initial faith. They will prove revolutionary!

---

[8] John C. Maxwell, *The 21 Indispensable Qualities of a Leader*, (Nashville TN.: Thomas Nelson, 1999), 3.

Paul follows Peter's lead by referring to the fruit of the Spirit (Gal 5:22–23). These attributes – which flow from the development of Christ-likeness as we allow the Spirit to control our lives – are essential in leadership. They speak of the necessary spirituality of the leader and remind us that spiritual development is a foremost priority. All leaders require a developing spiritual character, or one that is growing in line with the word of God as it works upon the heart and mind.

As you consider the call or desire for leadership; how is your character? Is it developing along God's lines? Who are you in God, in the presence of others, on your own? Before you proceed to know more about the mechanics of leadership a true character assessment is necessary. Return to Barnabas, a good man full of the Spirit and faith how do you measure up to that standard?

Why is this so important? As Maxwell writes:

Character brings lasting success with people![9]

Ultimately the leader must have successful relationships with others was seen in the life and ministry of Barnabas. The priority will be those who you lead but what about your success as a member of your family; do your family members know you for having an honest and stable character? What about people in your street: do they know you as an

---

[9] Maxwell, *21 Indispensable*, 3.

individual of good character? Can people depend on you, trust you, talk to you because they know your character is honest and upright?

As a leader you will go through situations, problems and good times which will be learning experiences; allow these to strengthen your character. If you go through things and don't learn the lessons from them and apply them to your life then the process has been wasted. God uses our trials to produce proven character, ask him to help you grow your character and don't simply recoil from the issues that have caused distress but learn from them and grow.

The first essential principle of Christian Leadership is to ensure you have a good, spiritual character. This should be based on the word of God and developed according to spiritual disciplines of Bible study and prayer. Also, don't be afraid to ask trusted friends or mentors how they think you are doing as you endeavour to develop your character.

Chapter 2: Clear Vision

> Where there is no prophetic vision the people cast off all restraint. Prov 29:18

Obtaining and pursuing a clear vision for the local church or para-church organisation is essential; this task falls to the leader(s). As the verse from Proverbs above reminds us; no vision leads to trouble. Unrestrained people end up doing whatever they want to or think best for them and not necessarily working for the greater good. However, a clear vision keeps everyone focussed on the task and allows for accountability amongst leaders and 'followers'. Oswald Chambers wrote:

> It is easier to serve or work for God without a vision and without a call, because then you are not bothered by what He requires. Common sense, covered with a layer of Christian emotion becomes your guide.[10]

Chambers' insight is seriously challenging; there are too many Christian 'leaders' carrying on with no vision and no accountability for their work. This is often because they are either not called to lead or not seriously seeking God in their calling. Common sense and emotion will not guide a church in the ways of God but will lead to a social group depending on a regular

---

[10] Oswald Chambers, *My Utmost for His Highest*, March 4th.

input of 'spiritual hype'. That is not to say that leaders don't require common sense or emotion, but they should never be the driving force or the decision making apparatus. It's God's way or no way! It's God's vision not human thinking.

It is necessary to lead in such a manner that others want to follow. This will occur when the leader has a clear vision, is passionate about it, people know it and don't want to get left behind. The leader with a divinely appointed vision will be so highly spiritually charged and pursuing the vision that others will simply follow. John Maxwell wrote:

> A great leader's courage to fulfil his vision comes from passion not position.[11]

Passion must drive the leader, this only comes from following a clear vision from God and being passionate about God and the gospel. Sadly, too many leaders want the position but are not interested in the passion of serving Jesus. This passion will arise from a vibrant relationship with Jesus and a clear vision from God. Such a vision and hence passion is only achieved by seeking God and his desires for your context. Your vision is not that of someone else who is being successful across town or in another country; it's what God wants for you in your situation. It is imperative that leaders do not try to live off someone else's vision

---

[11] Maxwell, *21 Indispensable*, 148.

but seek God for their own clear vision for the church community.

Why is vision so important?

The leader needs to be led, and their leader is God. God alone is the supplier of vision. Vision is a matter between you and God; don't go looking for it anywhere else. As the vision from God 'infects' you so you too will become infectious, others will catch the vision and run with it. Remember don't lose sight of that vision – it's God's given purpose and plan for you and so many others. Peter took his eyes of Jesus and sank in the waves, if you the leader take your eyes of Jesus you too could sink without trace.

Obtaining the vision

I mentioned earlier vision comes from God and through seriously seeking his plans and purposes.

1. As you start on the road of leadership take the whole situation to God in prayer; don't hold anything back your fears, desires, expectations, doubts, concerns about resources or lack of, needs, support network, simply everything that confronts you in your new challenge. Be honest with God and don't try to answer your prayers for him or pray the answers not the problems. God knows what you require and how long you need to wait for his answers. God desires for you to be relevant

in the context you are placed; if he's put you there, he will equip with vision and gifts to succeed.

2. Listen to God. Vision isn't about telling God what you want but waiting for him to speak into your situation and bring answers. Answers are only heard as you listen! Paul and his missionary team were guilty of wanting to go their own way as recorded in Acts 16:1–10. Their desire was to go to Asia then Bithynia however, God had a different destination in mind: Europe.

3. Don't rush into anything until you've had time to cogitate over the answers from God. Take your time and think through all the ideas you receive. You must be fully aware of all the possible difficulties you could confront on a practical and spiritual level as you make the vision known. Pray over the results of your thinking and promptings be sure you know it's God's will.

4. Don't be afraid to talk to a few well trusted and very carefully chosen advisors. It's good for leaders to have a mentor or confidant with whom to share their deepest desires and concerns. Often an outside perspective can have a dramatic effect on your thinking. Major decisions you make will affect a lot of people, your family, the church congregation and the wider community; godly input from other respected folk will prove invaluable. Also,

sometimes you don't need a response from someone simply a listening ear.

5. Formulate the vision and put it down on paper (or your tablet!). What is the main thrust of how you feel God is leading you and the direction he is pointing you and the church or organisation? When you see things in black and white, they become even more clear and help you push other ideas around that may compliment the overall vision.

6. Once you are certain, take it to the church leadership and await their response. Don't be surprised by indifference and opposition in the initial stages. Remember it took you time to get to the point of revelation; it will take time to get the leaders on board. However, this should not be too problematic if you have won their respect over previous years of ministry. That's why clear vision must come from a good character!

7. Take it to the church! Another round of questions, possible criticism, doubt, antagonism, negativity and ridicule. Remember if you know it's from God and you know it's the way ahead then stick to the task and carry the vision.

8. Don't wait too long to implement the vision. The initial stages can be introduced and then work with the church to implement the long-term strategy and goals. However, don't rush

it, take time to see each step set in place before moving on.

9. Evaluate at every stage of vision implementation, it's necessary to stop and consider where you've come from, where you are going and if the last step has been successful. Does anything need modifying, do you need to slow down or speed up the process?

10. Pray some more – always seek God to guide you every step of the way. Praying always is a divine injunction; never lose sight of the necessity of communicating with the vision provider. Once you've prayed, pray some more.

This 10–step outline is only a guide. I suggest it is a possible way forward in obtaining and implementing a new vision. I'm sure it could be added to, to be more effective, however I offer it as an outline for your consideration. However, there are a few words of caution before I leave this topic.

Caution an important principle in leadership.

1. Patience is essential when seeking a clear vision (Hab 2:3), yes it may take a little time, but God is always wanting to lead those who will genuinely seek his will.

2. Vision often begins very small, perhaps with an inner prompting, a desire, a concern which grows like an acorn into an oak. This inner

voice will be confirmed by the Word of God, the promptings of the Spirit, advice or confirmatory words from trusted people. As this grows it will burn in your heart and produce the passion require to move you and others to follow the vision. Luke 24:32–33 having listened to Jesus explain the Calvary event these 2 disciples couldn't wait to go and tell others of their saviour.

3. Vision doesn't have to be earth shatteringly different. It simply must be your vision from God for your context. Joshua had a great vision of what God wanted of him and the Israelites (Josh 1:7). Do what Moses did, and all will be fine. Vision may bring radical change, but it may not! Beware wanting to start a new vision by simply thinking everything must change. That's not a vision, it's a personal vendetta against anything from the past.

4. Seasons are real! Just as spring turns slowly into summer some visions end, and others begin. Don't cling on if something is 'dying'. Let it go and seek God for a new vision or direction for the new season (Eccl 3:1). I have found adopting this attitude of 'seasons' in spiritual life very helpful as it prevents me from clinging on to things for which I only have sentimental attachment. The church today does not require sentiment but the vision and purposes of God to be fulfilled in its leaders and members. Don't be afraid of

change but also don't go looking for it at every turn, if the vision God gives requires change then he will provide the opportunity for you to implement the change process. If change is necessary be confident, direct but sympathetic nobody likes change, and some will react negatively to even the suggestion of change. Be biblical, be God centred, be confident in God, be a sharer of vision and allow God to move on the people for his purposes.

Bill Hybels writes:

> Vision is at the very core of leadership. Take vision away from a leader and you cut out his or her heart. Vision is the fuel that leaders run on. It's the energy that creates action. It's the fire that ignites the passion of followers. It's the clear call that sustains focussed effort year after year, decade after decade, as people offer consistent and sacrificial service to God. [12]

Leadership requires a clear vision from God. As you consider your leadership role are you confident that God has given you clear vision for your context? If not, then purpose to set aside some quality time with God and seek his will for your situation. Find that quiet place, take your Bible a pen and paper and sit before

---

[12] Bill Hybels, *Courageous Leadership* (Grand Rapids: Zondervan, 2002), 31.

the Lord and ask him to prompt you in the right direction. Ask him to reveal his vision for the church to you. Don't look elsewhere; look to the Lord he will never disappoint.

Chapter 3: Commitment

Only be strong and very courageous, being careful to do according to all the law that Moses my servant commanded you. Do not turn from it to the right hand or the left, that you may have good success wherever you go. (Josh 1:7)

Joshua is encouraged to remain committed to the vision which he had received from God as he commenced the leadership of the people of Israel.

The leader must be 100% committed to the cause!

If the vision is real and the relationship to Jesus is vital, commitment shouldn't be an issue. Paul was a man committed to the cause despite all the difficulties he faced in his ministry; 2 Cor 11:23–33 is a catalogue of the opposition he faced as he endeavoured to serve the Lord and lead the church of Jesus Christ. However, despite this opposition he reminds king Agrippa in Acts 26:19 that he 'was not disobedient to the heavenly vision'. That's commitment; remaining faithful to the work even when faced with major opposition, discouragement, doubts, fears and inadequacies. What was Paul's vision? Simply Acts 26:16–18 to be a witness to Jesus Christ and preach the message of forgiveness of sin. Paul had one vision, one calling and one purpose – to follow Jesus and preach the gospel. He never relinquished his responsibilities.

Commitment is a major issue in society and something from which many people shy away. Commitment is lacking in relationships. People no longer look for lifetime partners. Commitment is lacking in employment, both with zero hours contracts and people not able to remain with the same employer for any length of time. These commitment issues have found their way into the church community. Membership is no longer viewed as being necessary as this leads to accountability. Pastors move from church to church once they've preached their stock of sermons. Congregants change churches in search of the latest fad in worship, the newest preaching sensation or a better brand of coffee! However, I submit that all this can change if the leader is committed, as this will slowly reflect in the members of the congregation. But, where does the leaders commitment focus? Three simple yet profound issues which I believe will enhance commitment in the leader and cascade through the congregation.

Commitment to Christ; People; Vision

Commitment to Christ

All leaders are first and foremost disciples of Jesus. "Follow me" wasn't simply a call to the original twelve disciples but to every subsequent individual who puts their faith in Christ. Following means discipleship which equates to a close spiritual walk with God. Paul tells Timothy in 1 Tim 4:12–16 to maintain this spiritual focus by paying attention to his spiritual disciplines.

Paul Beasley-Murray refers to this vital relationship, stating that:

> If pastors are to be successful in their role as leaders, they need to be God's men and women.[13]

If someone is God's man or God's woman then this will reveal itself not so much in their public profile as in their private devotion. Such areas of importance being personal prayer and Bible study, lifestyle, priorities, expectations and desires. Coupled with this, how the leader copes with disappointment, opposition, failure and criticism is also important. Leaders must focus on God and God's standards, allowing God's desires to be their desires and God's priorities to be their priorities.

The leader has a responsibility to themselves and the congregation to be looking firstly to Jesus. They must remain close to the Lord in their personal walk and be committed to the cause of the gospel, serving the Lord. As this becomes the norm for the leader so their commitment to the church community and hence the community's commitment to the Lord will grow and impact society. On the contrary, if the leader takes their eyes off Jesus and their personal walk falters they will suffer spiritually, the congregation will suffer spiritually, and the cause of the gospel will fail in their circle of influence. The quality of abiding in Christ

---

[13] Paul Beasley-Murray, *Dynamic Leadership*, (Eastbourne: MARC, 1990), 197.

(John 15:1–11) is of paramount importance. Spiritual life is received from the Lord due to that intimate relationship whereby spiritual life flows from the Lord. This prepares and keeps the leader in the role to which they have been called.

Leader, are you committed to Christ? Is he the centre of your affections and attentions or are there other things which interfere with the relationship you should have with Jesus? Why not resolve today to get back to that commitment you once had, prioritising your personal spiritual growth?

Commitment to People

All Christian leaders must be committed to the ones they are called to lead. In practice this means primarily being committed to their spiritual well-being and growth. Paul summaries this commitment in 2 Cor 11:28 as well as coping with the physical and mental abuse and turmoil he also writes of, "the daily pressure on me of my anxiety for all the churches." John Gill summaries Paul's concerns:

> and who continually stood in need of his watch and care over them, to provide ministers for some, to prevent schisms and heat divisions in others; to preserve others from errors and heresies, and warn them of the dangers to which they were exposed by false teachers; and to animate, strengthen, and support others under violent persecutions, lest their

faith should fail, and they be tempted to desert the Gospel, and drop their profession of religion.[14]

Every church leader faces similar anxieties as they brood over their charges; still today people have spiritual, emotional, physical and material needs; still today pastors and leaders stand in the gap on behalf of the congregation. Why because the love of God dwelling within causes the leader to want to serve the people and care for them as a shepherd cares for the flock (1 Pet 5:1–4). As Peter and Paul exhort us to remain committed to the people of God it is also good to notice their reason for this commitment:

> For now we live, if you are standing fast in the Lord. 1 Thess 3:8

Peter writes:

> For if these qualities are yours and are increasing, they keep you from being ineffective or unfruitful in the knowledge of our Lord Jesus Christ. 2 Pet 1:8

The Apostle John agrees:

> I have no greater joy than to hear that my children are walking in the truth. 3 John 4

Paul, Peter and John, the heavy-weights of New Testament writing, all had a desire for their readers, church members to grow in the Lord and to know his spiritual blessings. And, to receive that joy and life

---

[14] John Gill, 2 Corinthians 11:28 www.e-sword.net

within their own experiences. Leaders are you committed to the people of God to see them grow and to experience the joy and life of God in your own soul? Do you want the best for your congregation?

One's commitment can be measured by hearts and hands. Hearts that express that deep inner concern for the people of God in seeking their spiritual betterment. And hands in what you are prepared to do for the people of God. Some leaders operate a 'hands off' leadership style; whereas Jesus practiced an 'hands on' style. John 13:5 he washed the disciples' feet; an action which revealed his total commitment. Jesus demonstrated a true servant heart and attitude; unashamed of and unembarrassed by the menial task he undertook.

John Maxwell writes:

> People don't care how much you know until they know how much you care.[15]

Care, concern and commitment are all vitally and inextricably linked. It's not about how many college degrees you hold but how much you have a heart for people and how you demonstrate that care for people.

Leader; are you committed to the people of God? Do you care for God's people or are you someone who

---

[15] Maxwell, *21 Indispensable*, 103.

stands aloof from the people hoping someone else will do all the caring?

Commitment to Vision

The previous chapter dealt with the issue of vision and its importance in the life and experience of the leader. I am not going to retrace my steps here. Suffice to say that the leader must be committed to the vision granted to them by God. Seek the vision for you and the church community you lead, know it and implement it; then stick to it. Don't change until God tells you to take a turn in the road. Remember Joshua as mentioned at the start of this chapter; he was called to follow the vision that Moses had implemented and instructed not to deviate from the path because that was the way to success (Josh 1:8). Do you desire to have a successful ministry? Often, we are afraid to speak about success in the Christian ministry as we defer all our success to God. That is correct, nothing we achieve which is of lasting value comes from our own abilities, learning or natural gifts; it all comes from God. However, Joshua was told he would be successful as a leader if he followed God's vision, so why can't we be successful as leaders today? How is success measured? I believe there are two major measures of success:

1. Spiritual growth shown through spiritual fruit (Gal 5:22). The Spirit within causes these characteristics to blossom in one's life. This

should be visible to all as leaders and congregation grow spiritually.

2. Numerical growth in the church, as people come to faith and grow in their knowledge of the gospel. The church is being built by the Lord and we are to participate in the growth by proclaiming the gospel and seeing people changed and added to the church (1 Cor 3:6–9).

Commitment is a serious issue especially in an era where commitment is sadly lacking. Commitment to relationships is being side-lined, marriage and family commitments are being neglected. Work commitments are loose people look to change jobs every few years or even months. We live in a 'fad driven society' but there are no such thing as spiritual fads. The Bible calls for commitment to the cause of the gospel for the sake of the people of God. As a leader, don't look to jump from one church to another because someone has upset you or they offer a better employment package. Be committed to seeing the work of God through in the place he has called you, as you do you will know his blessing and enjoy an element of success.

Chapter 4: Complete Servanthood

> But made himself nothing, taking the form of a servant, being born in the likeness of men. Phil 2:7

Paul Beasley-Murray writes:

> The key to Christian leadership is servant-leadership. Servant-leadership focusses on the people to be cared for rather than just a job to be done.[16]

These words reflect the fact that Jesus was revolutionary in terms of his leadership style and expectations, for his primary objective was service. Perhaps this is best illustrated in two Bible passages, John 13:1–17 and Matt 20:20–28.

The incident in the Upper Room before the crucifixion best illustrates this revolutionary teaching; for the Rabbi, teacher, preacher, healer, Son of God, was willing to put aside his perceived status and wash the feet of the disciples. How willing are you to do the menial tasks in the church? Or are you someone who desires the praise for a 'great sermon' but is not interested in living out that sermon in a practical manner before the congregation?

---

[16] Beasley-Murray, *Dynamic*, 33.

John Maxwell writes:

> Servanthood is not about position or skill. It's about attitude … and the truth is that the best leaders desire to serve others and not themselves.[17]

How is this possible? It results from being a people person, recognising needs and potential in others. The true servant will identify needs and act to alleviate those needs. As potential in others is recognised the servant leader will teach them in such a way that they will fulfil that potential. Leaders should never desire the pre-eminence, authority, control and honour but should be serving God and their fellow humanity. Leadership is about perpetuating the work of God through others and setting an example of complete servanthood.

Jesus sets the benchmark for servant leadership for he established his ministry on the following principle:

> For the Son of Man did not come to be served, but to serve, and give his life as a ransom for many. Matt 20:28

This attitude is totally contrary to human thinking and understanding and further contrasts the natural and spiritual. In Matt 20:20–28 Jesus contrasts the areas of natural and spiritual, his emphasis is on a revolutionary paradigm of true leadership. Setting the scene, Jesus is asked by the mother of James and John

---

[17] Maxwell, *21 Indispensable*, 136.

that her sons may be preferred in the kingdom of God and given the positions of rank and power. This would have given them the prestige in the eyes of their mother and hopefully in the eyes of the other disciples. Was there a tension in the group between them and Peter, vying for the recognition as leader? However, Jesus turns the whole issue on its head by showing that they will have to endure suffering and service before they can ever think of positions of power and prestige. Ultimately, it is God alone who confers positions of prestige on people, all they need do as disciples is serve God and their fellow people. This is in complete contrast to the reasoning of the world where people seek out leadership to use the position and power for their own ends and the subjugation of others.

J. Oswald Sanders provides an interesting summary of the difference between natural and spiritual leaders:[18]

Natural	Spiritual
Self-confident	Confident in God
Knows men	Also knows God
Makes own decisions	Seeks God's will
Ambitious	Humble
Creates methods	Follows God's example
Enjoys command	Delights in obedience to God

---

[18] Sanders, *Spiritual Leadership*, 29.

Seeks personal reward   Loves God and others

Independent   Depends on God

Often with natural leadership people are there for the reward they receive and the prestige they attain. However, spiritual leadership seeks no earthly recognition or reward and simply focusses on the betterment of others. There are many Bible references to servant leadership, here are a few to consider:

In Acts 13:36, King David was simply a servant of his generation.

In Acts 20:18–21, Paul the Apostle was happy to serve the people (note the impact vv. 37–38).

In Rom 12:1, we find the call of all disciples is spiritual service, which is true worship.

In Gal 5:13, we see the standard of loving service for the disciples of Christ.

Phil 2:5–8 gives the example of Jesus for all to follow.

In Phil 2:19–23, Timothy was commended for his service.

The emphasis of the Christian faith is service towards humanity. When assessing leaders, they must be the ones who set the standard in the Christian community for service.

Complete servanthood is an example all leaders must take from the Lord himself. Peter sums this up in a very important passage. In 1 Pet 5:1–3 Peter emphasises the roles and responsibilities of the leader in respect to their example Jesus – the chief shepherd; he finishes his statement with one essential phrase; v 3 'be examples to the flock'. The true servant leader will demonstrate his/her leadership style in a positive manner to those they lead; a servant leader will have a church full of servant hearted disciples of Jesus. being an example is essential in Christian leadership, all are called to follow Christ:

Be imitators of me, as I am of Christ. (1 Cor 11:1).

Paul sets the standard here by stating that people can follow his example. However, there is an important caveat; only follow those who follow Christ. Hence, a godly example is essential in any leader and this is expressed in a variety of ways.

Paul continues his advice to Timothy a younger leader seeking to fulfil the purposes of God in his ministry:

Let no one despise you for your youth, but set the believers an example in speech, in conduct, in love, in faith, in purity. Until I come, devote yourself to the public reading of Scripture, to exhortation, to teaching. Do not neglect the gift you have, which was given you by prophecy when the council of elders laid their hands on you. Practice these things, immerse yourself in them, so that all may see your progress. Keep a close watch on yourself and on the teaching. Persist in this, for by so doing you will save both yourself and your hearers. 1 Tim 4:12–16

Paul's advice is essential reading for all leaders and should be a regular part of all leaders and potential leader's study. A few thoughts on this passage will suffice:

1. Age is no barrier to leadership and setting an example. Often in our churches we think only older people should be leaders. However, God can work in and through young people as well; Josiah was a young king, 8 years old, who caused great reform (2 Kings 22).

2. One's speech/language is a barometer of our inner self; what's inside is what comes out. The tongue is a very powerful member (Jas 3:1–12) its use can harm, spoil or encourage and edify.

3. The conduct of the leader is constantly under scrutiny, people see more than they hear, as you lead what do people see in your life? Where do you go, what do you do, how do you live? Are these things all glorifying to God? Col 4:5 reminds us to walk in a way that is helpful to those outside the church, wisdom is essential in one's conduct. Beware people are watching!

4. Love, faith and purity are three areas or spiritual virtues that the leader should excel in and that others can see and appreciate. The spiritual nature of the leader is essential and these issues link to one's character, as mentioned in chapter 1. Do you love God &

others, do you have faith in God and is the pursuit of purity high on your agenda?

5. The use of the Scriptures is a key element in leadership. One's understanding of and application of the word of God is vital in the leader's ministry. Paul encourages Timothy to promote the public use of the Bible because it is this teaching that helps strengthen people's faith (2 Tim 3:10–17).

6. Paul reminds Timothy that his ministry in leadership is a gift from God. All of us have gifts, and some are gifted to lead (Rom 12:6–8). However, leaders are also required to recognise gifts within others, as Paul did, and encourage them to flourish in the Lord's work.

7. The reminder comes to Timothy that leadership is a complete lifestyle. All these spiritual endeavours are things which the leader should immerse themselves in and concentrate attention on how they live. 24/7 leadership is essential. The leader cannot simply pick and chose when they want to be God's representative, it is a whole of life commitment.

8. Finally, Paul gives the reason for this servant/example setting attitude: salvation! Ultimately whatever the leader is involved in all should be done to promote the gospel and

the salvation of individuals. Are you a leader with a heart for the souls of people?

Setting an example as a servant of Jesus is essential in true biblical leadership. Are you willing to grasp the importance of the issue and set out to serve God and his people; his is a great commitment but worthwhile as eternal matters are at stake. One essential thought to keep in mind as you consider servant leadership is, 'Never ask someone to do something you wouldn't do yourself.'

As this becomes the default mind-set of the leader so too others will follow their lead and become complete servants of God.

As you contemplate leadership are you set on serving or ruling?

Chapter 5: Compassion

> But if anyone has the world's goods and sees his
> brother in need, yet closes his heart against him,
> how does God's love abide in him? 1 John 3:17

Love, concern, grace and mercy are key words to good
leadership. As mentioned earlier yet worth repeating,
Maxwell makes an excellent point:

> People don't care how much you know until they
> know how much you care.[19]

Maxwell is correct in his observation, we invest time,
effort and finance in preparing people for leadership
through learning the biblical principles, sending
people to Bible college, seminars and leadership gurus
but forget to encourage leaders to love! This love is a
divine deposit in one's heart and must be cultivated
and allowed to manifest itself in one's actions and
dealings with others. Developing a compassionate
nature is a key element in the process of leadership. If
love is the root of one's experience, then a
compassionate nature will follow. Paul deals with this
in Gal 5:22–26 where he lists the out-working of love in
the heart. Love and compassion should be a
benchmark for the leader's dealings with others. If
these virtues mentioned in Gal 5:22–26 are resident in

---

[19] Maxwell, *21 Indispensable*, 103.

the heart, then developing a compassionate and caring mind-set will be easier.

Peter confirms Paul's thinking in 2 Pet 1:5–11, where we notice that love is listed as a major element in the Christian life experience and is a virtue which can be developed. That is, it is possible for the individual to grow in their love for God and others. Peter calls attention to brotherly affection and emphasises how the Christian should have this true in-dwelling affection for others. Peter further warns of the consequences of not having these characteristics: unfruitfulness and barrenness in spiritual things. All leaders should desire to be fruitful and productive in their ministry and should have the desire to see others produce spiritual fruit. Compassion for others, devoting oneself to the personal growth of others is an imperative of the leader. Compassion and devotion to the people is essential and should not be disregarded by leaders.

Compassion, care and concern are inextricably linked to biblical Christian leadership. The leader must care for those under their oversight. This refers to the biblical pattern of shepherd leadership, where the shepherd's main concern is the well-being of the flock. Psalm 23 illustrates how the shepherd only wants what is good and beneficial for the sheep; good pastures, still waters, rest and a desire to protect. There is a deep need within the church for its leaders to love the people of God. Anyone who says they are a leader but does not love the people is going to struggle to win their confidence and therefore achieve anything for the sake of the gospel.

Compassion is seeing people's need and responding in a manner that will bring alleviation to the situation. Jesus once again sets the example of compassion Matt 9:36 he viewed the people's real need; spiritual direction and help. However, notice that compassion leads to action for Jesus implored the disciples to call on God to reap the harvest. There was a genuine concern that people were going to be lost if the disciples did not act in accordance with God's will and pray for workers to reach those under the burden of sin.

Compassion is possible in many areas of the life of the servant leader. Jesus is the ultimate example and it is good to examine his life and ministry to discover how he demonstrated compassion.

In Mark 1:41, we see compassion on the outcasts in society.

Mark 5:19 reveals his compassion on the lost; the call to personal evangelism.

In Mark 8:2, we note Jesus' compassion due to physical circumstances.

In Matt 11:28–30, we find that Jesus had compassion on those struggling with the weight of religion.

Luke 23:34 shows Christ's compassion for his enemies.

Also, Luke 23:42–43 indicates Christ's compassion for the guilty yet repentant.

Beasley-Murray writes:

> Love not only initiates and sustains the service of the Christin leader, it also provides the basis for a leader's authority… The authority of leaders in such a setting (church) lies in their love for the people. It is as people begin to discover and experience his/her love for them, that they in turn allow him/her to have authority over their lives, both individually and corporately. Confidence and trust in leaders develop in proportion to the extent to which leaders are perceived to love their people.

Beasley-Murray continues:

> Leaders who love their people will do their best to encourage those in their care…

> Leaders who truly love their people will be unafraid to speak the truth in love…

> Leaders who love their people will always have time for individuals.

> Such love will prove effective in achieving the task, building the team, and meeting the needs of individuals.[20]

Do you love the people of God?

---

[20] Beasley-Murray, *Dynamic*, 192–194.

How do you demonstrate compassion to those in the church community?

1 Cor 13 lists how all disciples and especially leaders should love.

1 Cor 13: A summary

This chapter is so often relegated to a wedding reading; however, it must be considered in its correct context. Paul is dealing with a church in turmoil, especially in relation to the operation of spiritual gifts. There are all sorts of moral issues contaminating the life of worship and he focusses the congregation's attention by dealing with the heart of Christianity: 'love'. Further, this chapter is not intended to advocate the position of love over that of spiritual gifts; gifts are not redundant but should function within a loving context. Paul is illustrating here how all ministry should emanate from love, should be controlled by love, and be carried out in a loving manner. If one examines true spiritual ministry the watchword is love and 1 Cor 14:40 gives the motive – building up the church. Spiritual ministry then is not measured by one's abilities or gifts but by the love that is within and works out through one's life and ministry. All we desire to achieve as leaders must be for the common good; what do these different aspects, both positive and negative, reveal as being at the heart of the true leader. This is a key chapter that requires a little more attention.

V.1 Paul states if whatever one says comes from a heart with no love then the person is simply making a hollow and offensive noise! A noise rather than true instruction; a noise which is distracting and not helpful. However, if your life is centred on the love of God then your spiritual gifts will have a good impact. Leaders must set the standard for what they say and how they say it will cascade to the congregation.

V.2 Faith here is the most powerful demonstration of God's power working through an individual. Here we see that some of the most powerful effects of faith are possible and necessary as God can miraculously change people's situations. However, the vehicle through which God works must be love. Divine power is not desired simply for one's personal boasting, power should be sought in a loving manner to change people for the good.

V.3 Generosity a biblical principle that should not be overlooked; we have a responsibility to show philanthropic help to those around us. Leaders should set the example in the area of giving which is a key biblical message. Are you a generous leader? The congregation will only respond in a manner that they see in their leader's generosity is essential; giving of time, emotion and finance. However, Paul states that even the greatest sacrifice must stem from a heart of love.

V.4 Patience is the passive side of love, long forbearance with others. Leaders must learn patience.

This will be particularly important as you deal with the wrongs and personal injuries suffered. People are always happy to denounce the leader, but with patience you can cope with the criticism, quarrels, opposition and frustrations. Remember that patience does not mean allowing sin in the church to go unchecked; if something is wrong then deal with it, it may take time to break through but with patience you can do it (2 Tim 2:24–26).

Kindness is the active side of love. This is goodness on behalf of others or demonstrating love in action. Often as a leader you will spend much time in talking, teaching, preaching but there comes a time for action. Graham Scroggie said, 'You can no more have love without kindness as you can have springtime without flowers'.[21] Kindness is the willingness to go and help others, to relieve burdens, to support, to be practical; kindness is 'love in work clothes'![22]

The absence of envy and jealousy shows that love demonstrates no rivalry – a common problem in church life and especially within leadership circles (1 Cor 3:3). Never be resentful or envious of another's gifts or success as this can be destructive.

The absence of boasting reveals that love is not self-centred. It does not lead us to boast about our personal

---

[21] Cited in Alexander Strauch, *Leading with Love*, (Colorado: Authentic 2006), 44.
[22] Strauch, *Leading*, 44.

spirituality, gifts and qualities. Too many leaders think too highly of themselves and let other people know it they crave attention (Prov 27:2).

Love is not proud or arrogant: Like the previous boasting, being 'puffed up' means thinking too highly of yourself, believing that you are better than others. Don't be a limiter of people because you think you know it all!

V.5 Love is not rude or unbecoming. It does not behave shamefully or with a bad attitude either in public or in private. The leader should not act in an inappropriate manner but should adhere to standards of decency and order; appearance, subject of conversation, language used, ignoring other people's ideas, thoughtless actions, inappropriate behaviour with the opposite sex and being discourteous to others.

Love is not self-seeking. It does not seek self-promotion or self-gain. We live in a very selfish society, which cries, 'me first'! This does not translate into a loving Christian community where Christ always put others first (2 Cor 12:14–15).

Love is not easily angered/provoked. Those around can sometimes say or do things which make the leader angry however the leader must be very careful not to be angered too quickly. This relates to patience, if one starts with a patience the exterior issues will not cause an inappropriate quick-tempered response that can lead to further disruption (Luke 6:29–31).

Love keeps no record of wrongs/not resentful or holds a grudge. The Christian leader should never desire to see others who may have done wrong against them suffer retribution. Never desire evil against someone even when they are known to be wrong. Don't keep a record of wrongs and await vengeance. Forgiveness is key (Eph 4:32).

V.6 Love does not delight in evil/rejoice in unrighteousness: Any sort of evil impure practice should repulse the Christian and the leader must set the example. Avoid the filth that is easily available in the world and don't gossip about others that is unnecessary. There is a necessity for leaders to show the way in keep things pure (Eph 4:25–31).

Love rejoices in truth: The exact opposite to the previous statement. Love wants what is good, right and true and is glad when the truth wins (3 John 3–4).

V.7 Love bears all things/protects. There is nothing that love cannot face, and it will stand up for others. Life has some heavy loads but with the love of God at the centre we can cope. This is supremely true of the leader. There will be a lot to bear in the life of service; don't give up under the strain remember love for people keeps you focussed and love for God keeps you going (Gal 6:2).

Love believes all things/always trusts. The loving leader will never cease to have faith in God and others. Believe the best in everyone and have a deep-seated faith in God. Faith keeps us going! All rests on the Lord (Phil 1:6).

Love always hopes/hopes all things: Love centred on God never loses hope even when situations you face may humanly appear hopeless; where Jesus is there is always hope! Note Paul's words of confidence in (2 Cor 7:16).

Love endures all things/perseveres. Love will bring a tenacity to one's life. As leaders, you will have to face all sorts of nonsense, attitudes, criticism and questions but love endures all the rubbish for the sake of growing the people of God. As 2 Cor 11:23–12:9 shows, whatever you face grace is available.

V.8 Love never fails, it is eternal, permanent. When all these human deficiencies are dealt with, when one day we will no longer bicker, argue, criticise and doubt we will realise that it was love that was the over-riding power that kept us going.

V.13 Love is the greatest because God is love (1 John 4:8).

Paul is demonstrating in these verses the superiority of love and its supreme characteristics; these should be applied to all Christian lives especially leaders. Compassion is vital.

Chapter 6: Courage

> So take heart, men, for I have faith in God that it will be exactly as I have been told. Acts 27:25

Karl Barth wrote, 'Courage is fear that has said its prayers'.[23] This is a very interesting perspective on courage, for it highlights how fear can often be the uneasy partner to Christian leadership. However, the leader must be courageous, so what is courage? Collins dictionary defines it thus:

> Courage is the power or quality of dealing with or facing danger, fear, pain etc… the courage of ones' convictions is the confidence to act in accordance with one's beliefs.[24]

How as a leader may you have to face danger, fear or pain and remain firm in your belief? Many situations will come across your path as a leader having courage or facing these difficulties with a firm faith in God's calling and equipping will be necessary. Hence, a strong and deep faith in God is a vital prerequisite of Christian leadership.

Courage often means that the individual will have to face tough decisions and take a great step of faith believing that God is with them and his plans and purposes are the way forward.

---

[23] Maxwell, *21 Indispensable*, 37.

[24] Collins English Dictionary.

Maxwell gives some interesting points on courage:

1. *Courage Begins with an Inward Battle.* Every test you face as a leader begins within you... Courage isn't an absence of fear. It's doing what you are afraid to do. It's having the power to let go of the familiar and forge ahead into new territory.

2. *Courage Is Making Things Right, Not Just Smoothing Them Over.* Great leaders have good people skills and they can get people to compromise and work together. But they also take a stand when needed. (The leader must know when to stand up for their convictions; potential to move and change is far more important than appeasement).

3. *Courage in a Leader Inspires Commitment from Followers.* A show of courage by a leader inspires. It makes people want to follow.

4. *Your Life Expands in Proportion to Your Courage.* Fear limits a leader. But courage has the opposite effect. It opens doors, and that's one of its most wonderful benefits. Courage not only gives you a good beginning, but it also provides a better future.[25]

What do you think of Maxwell's comments on courage and how do you need to be courageous as you lead? I submit that these suggestions on courage are worth re-

---

[25] Maxwell, *21 Indispensable*, 40–41.

reading and allowing them to settle in one's heart and mind. Let's unpack some of Maxwell's ideas and see how they can apply to biblical leadership.

The inward battle. As you contemplate the spirituality of biblical leadership it is necessary to understand that the inward battle has a spiritual as well as natural dimension. Ephesians 6:10–13 highlights this important factor. Our fear may be due to lack of self-belief – 'can I do that task?' However, in the spiritual realm it may be that our fears result from satanic opposition. Hence it is vital to realise that the battle or wrestling is not in the flesh but in the spiritual realm. I return to the necessity of all leaders being spiritually minded and focussed on spirituality which will enhance all the courageous steps they have to take. Paul encourages the Ephesian believers to take hold of the spiritual armour or the wherewithal provided by God to assist us in these fear full battles. The inward battle can only be won as the inner person is strengthened in the spiritual realm. It is also relevant to recognise here that in Eph 6 after Paul has listed the so called 'Christian's Armour' he encourages his audience to be constantly engaged in prayer, of which more later.

Making right, not smoothing over. Truth is more necessary than peace. As a leader you will be confronted with difficult decisions which may affect others and upset them in their lives. However, the stand for biblical truth is vital as a biblical leader should lead by biblical principles. If an issue is unbiblical then it must be dealt with. I would agree with Maxwell that compromise is sometimes necessary, but it is not always the best way forward. This is particularly true when dealing with the two people's different ideas of how to approach a situation where both may be acceptable. However, when there is a definite biblical standard of right or wrong compromise must never be the solution. As a courageous leader it will be necessary to make a stand for the correct biblical principle for truth always succeeds over peace. Too many churches and Christians have been damaged by lack of courage in the decisions of their leaders. Furthermore, unscrupulous individuals will engage in seeking compromise to avoid admitting they were wrong. Leaders need courage and discernment to approach often delicate situations and bring a resolution that is biblical and godly.

Courage inspires others: All leaders are judged by how many are following and how enthusiastic these followers are in their commitment to the vision. Often people respond to courageous leadership even if they make mistakes. Inspiring others to serve and then hopefully to lead themselves is a key element of leadership. Paul encouraged Timothy to copy his way of life and leadership skills (2 Tim 2:1–2). The opposite is also true when people see fear in a leader, they are more prone to avoid them and their suggestions as this fear affects faith. As you think about your leadership role do you desire to inspire others by being an example of courage in God. This does not mean that the leader is loud mouthed and brash or even arrogant but willing to take God at his word and do the right thing even if it may be unpopular. Following God courageously will not fit well with everyone but will inspire others of a godly disposition.

Your life expands in proportion to your courage: It may be better put that one's faith grows as you take courageous steps in God. As you see God work in your life then you are more liable to trust him for the next courageous decision you need to make. Many live with disappointment because they are not willing to believe God and step out in faith, and then step out again when he prompts them to move. This faith returns us to the issue of a vital relationship with God as the driving force of true biblical leadership. A life of faith, with complete trust in God to lead, guide, direct and keep will allow the leader to grow and make a greater impact for God (Jas 1:6; Heb 12:1–3; Acts 27:22–25).

Are you ready and willing to take that giant step? Do you have the courage to stand up for what you believe to be right and go forward in a belief that God is at the back of all you do? You may not be the most popular person if you take courageous steps and decisions that affect the lives of others. Most don't want to be shifted from their comfort zones, they don't want to be challenged about their lifestyle choices. They don't want to face the fact that God knows best. However, as a leader you need to exhibit great courage in tackling difficult situations – that may just be the thing that unlocks the blessing of God in the congregation. Courage comes as the leader is close to God and knows divine guidance; this isn't simply shouting the loudest it's knowing God's will and purpose. We are in a spiritual battle, and the soldier who does not display courage will fail and be defeated as well as cause fellow soldiers to doubt, fear, and retreat.

Courage is not being 'pig-headed' or stubborn it's having a certainty in the revelation of God. Often leaders must be courageous in their public ministry due to unsavoury situations that arise in the church community and the wider-world. If as a leader you have implicit trust in God, then dealing with these unsavoury situations will not be easy but it will be divinely directed. As Paul counselled the leader Timothy, he gave him some sound advice about courageous leadership (1 Tim 1:3–4; 4:6,7,12–16; 2 Tim 2:14, 24–26). The leader's courage is not in themselves or in their ability but purely in the revealed word of God for any given situation. A courageous leader is a leader steeped in the Bible one who knows how to apply biblical principles in trying situations.

Someone once said: 'Never doubt in the dark what God has revealed to you in the light'.

This is a great adage for the courageous leader; be close to God, listen to him, know his ways and then taking those steps of faith will not be quite so daunting.

Be a courageous leader; take God at his word and go for it!

Chapter 7: Communication

Pray, then like this: 'Our Father in heaven, hallowed be your name.' Matt 6:9

'It's good to talk', and the leader who doesn't communicate is going to fail! The Christian leader who doesn't talk is going to fail and has the potential to spiritually ruin a congregation. There are 2 vital areas of communication for the Christian leader: communication with God and communication with people.

Communicating with God

Leaders must talk to God, for this is the main line of communication between the chief architect of the church and the builders. Instruction, vision, and direction can only come from God, and this is what the church needs if it is going to be what God intends it to be within a given context.

Prayer is essential for the leader, for if you don't pray you can't properly lead (Ps 77; Matt 6:5–6). The leader should set the example in this spiritual discipline; the world needs a praying church and the church needs praying leaders. Set the example of communication with God. Beasley-Murray states that the leader must commune with Jesus because he is the source of example, strength and direction.[26] As the leader receives these graces from the Lord, so they too can demonstrate them and encourage them amongst the people they lead. A personal example here is a great illustration. My father was a pastor for many years. As a young person I have vivid memories of dad in his study at prayer. This has stuck with me for over 40 years and I know that his example has taught me the importance of seeking God. Of regularly setting aside time to get close to God and know his will and direction in my life and the life of those I have been privileged to lead. Being a praying leader is the path to success.

The spiritual dimension of leadership is again seen in the necessity of prayer. This is the most powerful weapon in the armoury of the Christian and should be vital to all leaders.

The words of Matt 6:5–6 are essential in understanding prayer. Here we read of the necessity of private prayer. It is no good for leaders to confine their praying to public demonstrations, generally in gatherings of the congregation or at the bedside of the sick. Effective prayer takes place in the secret place, in the quietness. Never think that time spent in prayer is time wasted. As leaders it is essential to prioritise personal prayer and that includes prayer for self and for those you lead. We live in a non-stop society where we believe that we

---

[26] Beasley-Murray, *Dynamic,* 200–205.

must always be doing something. Prayer is doing something! It's communing with God on behalf of the people entrusted to your care. Set aside quality time to pray; don't rush through your prayer list but take time to think and pray for individuals, ministry topics, situations, and concerns. Remember to thank God for his help, to praise him for his goodness and answered prayers. Paul highlights this in Phil 4:6-7; we are prone to be anxious about situations and people problems however the antidote is prayer and thanksgiving. Notice the peace comes not from having the answer you desire but from simply taking that petition to the Lord in prayer. Are you a leader who can take your cares to the Lord and leave them there and receive his peace that he is going to deal with your request in his time and for his purposes? Paul continues to instruct the Colossians in a similar vein in Col 4:2, where he speaks about earnest prayer or to 'continue in' prayer. This is an encouragement to be permanently committed to praying and as Jesus said in Luke 18:1, we should always pray and never give up. It can be tempting to give up on situations because we see no immediate answer. God wants us to continue to pray because often prayer involves not so much him providing the answer we desire but him changing our wills to fit in with his perfect plans; this can take time!

If you are called to lead, you are called to pray because it is necessary for the church to be led the way God wants it to go; his way. Jeremiah reminds us of this essential aspect (Jer 29:11-13). Seeking God is unavoidable for the true leader of God's people. As a leader are you intent on seeking God's plans and purposes? You cannot afford to lead without God's direct communication. Resolve to pray more, to seek God, to take people and situations to God in prayer this is where the battle is won or lost.

The New Testament epistles reveal something about how Paul, the major leader of first century Christianity, prayed. Here are a few examples of the Apostle Paul's prayers:

2 Corinthians 13:7 – praying for others that they may live correctly and know the difference between right and wrong. Paul has a concern for the general spiritual health of the Corinthians as he was concerned that he would have to visit them with a word of correction. However, if the leader prays for the people that they will do the right thing and avoid the immoral or non-biblical way then their ministry will not be corrective but aimed at building up. Do you pray that people will know and do the right things?

Ephesians 1:15–23 – this is a magnificent prayer for people from the leader Paul. Here he focusses on their spiritual needs and growth in the things of God. Firstly, he thanked God for all the people (Philemon 4). How thankful are you today for the people has called you to lead? Secondly, he prays that they will have the wisdom and revelation of God in their hearts and minds. How desperately the church needs God's wisdom as an ever-present guide! Are you praying for people to know his wisdom and have a knowledge of and from him? In v. 18 Paul then seeks their spiritual enlightening; again, the spiritual dimension of his desire for them is obvious and necessary. As a leader are you regularly praying for the spiritual advancement of the people of God? This prayer is far removed from the usual, 'I'll pray for your migraine' type of prayers so many people engage with for others.

Ephesians 3:14–19 is another exquisite prayer from Paul for the disciples at Ephesus. Receive an inner strength from God that will come from the Spirit of God working within you and experience the love of God in a fuller measure. This love has such great dimensions, reaches so far, and encompasses the world, that the individual can never totally comprehend it; however, pray that people's hearts will be able to receive and know more of the love of God. What greater prayer could you make for the people of God than to know God's love in a greater manner? Are you praying spiritual prayers for God's people?

Continuing this great theme of prayer in Ephesians we come to 6:18–20. Here Paul encourages the people to pray constantly but especially for the opportunities for him to witness (see also Philemon 6). A leader must be willing to demonstrate a certain amount of vulnerability. Paul needed prayer as much as anyone. Encourage the congregation to pray constantly (1 Thess 5:17), and to pray for you as you lead.

Communicating with Others

The leader must communicate with others; firstly, with the church board/council and then with the congregation. This allows for the cascading of the vision for the church and gets everyone to the position that they are all, 'singing from the same hymn sheet' and not doing their own thing. Therefore, it is necessary to connect with others, to build relationships with others in the church is a vital aspect of good leadership. Beasley-Murray writes:

> The good leader, we have argued, 'works as a senior partner with others to achieve the task, build the team, and meet individual needs.' Leadership, according to this definition, involves working with others.[27]

Working with others and having good relationships is essential. It is not good to try and work with people but avoid a relationship with them. Make friends of your fellow workers, get to know them and their families, understand their background, desires, needs and work with them as a fellow human being and be a friend to them this will lead to openness in conversation, trust, respect and accountability (something which is often lacking in church leaders). As you get to know other leaders, workers, and congregants then this will allow for mutual respect, encouragement and lead to greater loyalty and deeper relationships. Work at your

---

[27] Beasley-Murray, *Dynamic*, 43.

relationships this will only be achieved as you communicate with people express your heart to them let them see where you are in God and let them see your vulnerabilities; remember you are not perfect.

As the church moves forward it must move together. If the vision of the church is not communicated to the congregation then there will be no support for the ministry. This is particularly important when considering new ministry ventures. Vision needs the support of the people of God, but if they don't know what the vision is and why it is being suggested, then you cannot expect them to get on board and throw their efforts, time and money into any work. Consult with the church, talk to the church about how God has brought you the vision, be honest about possible hurdles you may all face, but express your heart in such a way that they too will catch the fire of God's plans and purposes. Be a good communicator both from the front of the church but also in private. Be clear about what God is saying to you and move forward in his will.

Joshua was such a leader. Joshua 1:6–9 offers a direct revelation from God about how to lead. Interestingly, it contains nothing drastically new, but simply exhorts Joshua to follow the path of Moses! We don't all always have to innovate. Sometimes God simply says keep doing what you are doing, it's my path to success. Joshua 3 illustrates how this new leader spoke confidently to the people about God's plans and the way forward. In verse 5, he says prepare your selves spiritually – all we do in church life must have a spiritual foundation. Verse 6 teaches us never move without God's presence. The Ark of the Covenant was the symbol of God's presence with them, the pillar of cloud and fire were no more, and so they needed to trust in God's word and his presence. Joshua directs the people to the word of God (v. 9), without which all Christian ministry is doomed to failure. Joshua was a successful leader because he heard from God and told the people where and why they were going in a certain direction. Are you a leader who has the mind of God for your situation? If so, are you communicating it to the people of God? A good biblical leader will know God and his plans and will be able to cause people to follow the truth as revealed in the word of God.

Chapter 8: Complementarity

> Get Mark and bring him with you, for he is very useful to me for ministry. 2 Tim 4:11

To complement someone means that you or someone else completes something or someone. Do you have a spirit that allows for others to complete what is lacking in your ministry and leadership?

In the text above (2 Tim 4:11), Paul provides some insights into his heart. Firstly, he recognised his earlier mistake. Acts 15:36–41 records how Paul did not want Mark to be a part of the ministry team due to an earlier issue. However, with time and a humble spirit Paul now recognised Mark's qualities and worth. As a leader never be afraid to recognise that people change, and that forgiveness is a real part of life and leadership. Mark went on to be a great help in Paul's ministry and of course, wrote a gospel history of the life of Jesus. Who has never faltered, wobbled a little when confronted with a new challenge or been overwhelmed by the pressure of ministry? Mark was, you have been and will be in the future. Recognise that we all make mistakes for a variety of reasons. Have the humility to seek restoration for that person who you think has let you down; there could be a John Mark in the making. Secondly, Paul realised that Mark could do things that he couldn't, and so he was a useful addition to the team. Whether this was to put the finishing touches to the gospel story, to preach, or to simply make the tea what matters is he was needed by Paul. Look around your congregation – is there someone who has disappointed you, perhaps deserted you at a crucial time, criticised your style, ministry or lack of visitation? Go to them talk to them and see if they can get back on board to help you lead; perhaps freeing you from some responsibility which you don't need to hold – even making the tea! Mark complemented Paul in some aspect of ministry, and there are people out there waiting for you to recognise that you can't do it all on your own and that they can help you move forward in ministry. Reach out to them and work together for the sake of the kingdom of God.

A major strength of a good leader is recognising one's weaknesses! It is not failure to admit you have a weakness in one area or another. We all have strengths and weaknesses. Sadly, too many leaders emphasise the strengths but avoid the weaknesses. Complementarity involves being confident in who you are as a leader and recognising you need others to support your ministry in your weaker areas.

As an effective leader; you must be a team player! Are you?

However, before you can get there you must recognise and accept your weaknesses. Have you done so?

Why do you fear admitting a weakness in your ministry, character or knowledge? Why not be honest with God today and focus on a weakness you need the Lord to help you with by providing a supporter.

Are you willing to seek the help and input of others to complement your ministry? Look around where do you need help and who can be the answer to your dilemma?

Teamwork is essential to strong churches. You cannot have a 'one man show' whereby the pastor/leader dominates every aspect of church life. Yes, as we have said, they should bring the vision to the church. However, they must not assume overall control or be allowed to assume overall control by others. The leader must recognise they do not have all the gifts and others must be employed to share the load and fill in the gaps in their ministry. For example, all pastors should be able to teach, however not all pastors are great Bible expositors. Hence a pastor should seek others to complement their preaching ministry. Some are not so good at visiting or dealing with young people, so, find someone else in the Christian community who can help with such ministries. However, never shirk your responsibilities! You must work on your weaknesses and improve yourself in God to be a better teacher/preacher/visitor etc.

All God's people are gifted to be used in some aspect of ministry (Eph 4:11–12); this I believe, is to prevent leaders become autocrats and dictators. One should also notice that the reason for these ministry gifts is to equip everyone for works of service or ministry in the Christian and wider communities. Too often churches appoint a pastor/leader and leave everything to them. 'We pay them so let them get on with the work', is a common attitude. Their work is to equip others to do the work and to complement the ministry of that employed or appointed leader. Beasley-Murray states:

> The clear implication is that every Christian has a part to play if the body is to function properly.[28]

This is a biblical principle that all leaders would do well to put into practice; build a team of people who complement your ministry, to support you and correct you in your ministry. This is known as the art of delegation and is a very important leadership survival plan, J. Oswald Sanders writes:

> One facet of leadership is the ability to recognize the special abilities and limitations of others, combined with the capacity to fit each one into the job where he or she will do best. To succeed in getting things done through others is the highest type of leadership.[29]

I would go further than Sanders here, and state that it is also necessary for the leader to recognise their own special abilities and limitations and to find others to complement them in their ministry. Focus on your strengths but do not neglect your weaknesses and work on them to improve yourself and make yourself a more rounded leader.

---

[28] Beasley-Murray, *Dynamic*, 47.

[29] Oswald Sanders, *Spiritual Leadership*, 137.

The 'Body of Christ' analogy that Paul uses in 1 Cor 12 provides essential reading for the issue of giftedness in the church. This is also supported by Rom 12:2, where Paul refers to different people with different gifts complementing each other in the ministry of the local church. God gives the gifts and abilities which are wide ranging; however, it falls to the leaders to allow these gifts to be nurtured and used. Never see someone else's gifts as a challenge to your authority and leadership, but rather see them as a means of growing the church of God. In 1 Cor 12:28–30 Paul recognises that we are all different with different gifts but that is not a reason to look at those gifts as a badge of spiritual superiority. They are, instead, a means of grace to help others. As Paul continues his discourse on gifts and the body of Christ his famous chapter on love is pivotal, 1 Cor 13 is not a wedding reading but a challenge to serving one another in love by using the gifts and abilities God has given us. Ultimately this is summarised in 1 Cor 14:26 in that whatever is done must be done to build up our fellow disciples. Are you using your gift to build others up? Leaders, are you happy to recognise the gifts in others and promote them in ministry especially in areas where you struggle? If you do this will produce a stronger church and a more effective ministry.

Teamwork: A Summary.

The reasons for teamwork are:

I)   It spreads the load of responsibility. Moses (Exod 18:13–27) accepted advice about this even though he was the great leader.

II)   It provides accountability hence avoiding total control (cf. Paul and Peter in Gal 2:1–14).

III)   Provides security (Mark 6:7–13; Luke 10:1; Acts 13:2–3).

IV)   Supplements one another. Paul needed help from John Mark (2 Tim 4:11).

V)   Provides encouragement leadership can be a lonely place (2 Tim 1:16–17)!

It is essential that the strong leader recognises their weaknesses and employs every means to complement their leadership and ministry for the advancement of God's kingdom on earth through the local church.

Be honest about yourself and your weaknesses. Don't think you have to be 'Superman' or 'Wonderwoman'. Gather around you a group of godly servants who will allow you to fulfil your potential whist they fulfil theirs. Seek help, support, advice and encouragement from a team who want to serve the Lord and his people.

Chapter 9: Confidentiality

Let what you say be simply 'Yes' or 'No'; anything more than this comes from evil. Matt 5:37.

As a leader you will be expected to keep issues confidential. People will come to you with major life issues that require serious conversation and action. You must never publicise someone's secret concerns to the whole world! There are things which are said behind closed doors that only the person, you and God should know about.

In modern society people are confronted with a variety of serious issues, pornography, sexuality, debt, alcohol, relationships, harassment, or abuse, these all require sensitivity and confidentiality. Often the area concerns moral choices which must be biblically based as you counsel people with any of these or other major personal issues, remember they are personal and should be treated as confidential. However, depending on the issue under discussion, it may be necessary to bring in other help or support. However, unless in cases where an individual is at risk, such as when an allegation of child abuse is made, never do this until you have discussed it with the individual concerned. Obviously, if a vulnerable adult or child is at risk of abuse, the appropriate authorities (police, social services) should immediately be contacted.

This is where complementarity comes into view again. It is necessary to know where you need help, is there a counsellor who specialises in certain areas that can help, is there a medical person in the church who could offer advice? As a leader you will be expected to have all the answers but don't forget God has placed in the body many gifts that you as a leader can utilise.

Do not be a gossip, especially when you use the pretext that you were sharing the news, so others could pray. If the individual concerned wants to tell others, then leave that to them – it is not your place to open your mouth about other people's problems. A shallow concern for others is not the correct attitude if there is a genuine concern then there will be a genuine desire for confidentiality. (*or anywhere !!!*)

More problems are caused in local churches due to a loose tongue than to any other reason. The leader must never talk about the confidential issues either of personal situations or of disagreements in the church board/council. This can lead to great upset, discord, and eventually division.

James 3:1–12 sets out this point very strongly. The tongue can be used to stir up fires that cause major problems. What is often overlooked in this text is that James is talking to or about leaders and or potential leaders or teachers. It is those with the authority to teach and hence lead that must be especially careful with how they use their tongues. The words of a teacher/leader have tremendous weight in the local church community, and therefore care must be taken when opening one's mouth, particularly when instructing from the word of God. Never use the pulpit as an opportunity to bully others to come around to your way of thinking; and never use it as a public platform to deal with private issues. Be careful what you say and where you say it as it can have devastating effects upon innocent people. If there is a major concern that needs to be dealt with there is a biblical prescription found in Matt 18:15–17 that should be followed. As a leader/teacher you are the one who should set the standard of confidentiality but also of dealing correctly with misdemeanours in the congregation.

How do you see Jas 3:1–12 as being important in your situation?

Do you endeavour to keep a guard over your tongue?

Consider what you can do to help develop an attitude of confidentiality.

Another aspect of confidentiality is ensuring that your word is your word; as leaders we must never be seen to go back on our word (Matt 5:37; Jas 5:12). The integrity of the leader is essential – a simple 'yes' or 'no' should suffice for people to accept your word. The righteous person's word should be sufficient, and the leader should follow through on their word by correct and relative actions. Therefore, when a discussion is had, a decision made, or a judgment passed do not then talk to others and contradict yourself. Stand firm on your word and your decision and ensure that people know where you stand and that you can be trusted. A vital and often overlooked factor is that when we say anything God is the silent listener to every conversation and as Jas 3:1 reminds us leaders will be judged with a 'greater strictness'. Can you afford to have the judgement of God hanging over you because you have let the issue of confidentiality slip?

Have you been in a situation where you have gossiped about someone in the name of 'sharing concerns'?

Do you guard your tongue to ensure no harm is caused to others in your care?

Remember the old rabbinical saying; 'you have two ears always open to listen and one tongue kept behind a wall of teeth'. Let's be eager to listen, but not so eager to speak about the issues which we leaders must face.

I have become very concerned about the amount of lying which takes place in the body of Christ. There is no place for lying in the Christian life (Col 3:9). This is a severe ethical issue, and as leaders we should never be found to have lied about anything in our ministry or in the life of the church or any individual. The whole issue of lying is concerned with deception, false promises, honesty, integrity, openness and commitment to the truth. God never lies and cannot lie so his representatives on earth should never be involved in lying or deception. One of the names of the devil is the 'deceiver' and he is known as 'the father of lies' (John 8:44). This is a very serious issue, for if lying has a demonic source then it should have no part in the Christian life. Sadly, people justify lies by categorising them as 'little lies' or 'white lies' when there is no such thing. Any lie is a deception and as leaders we are not there to deceive but to deal in truth and honesty. We often forget the consequences of such unwholesome words and actions, including possible exclusion from the eternal state (Rev 21:27). The condition of Christianity in the West is such that the church has lost sight of the eternal purposes of God. Local empire building has replaced church mission, stepping on anyone and everyone to get position, power and authority has led to lies and deception filling many churches. This must stop because it is destructive and detrimental to spiritual growth and forgets the eternal purpose of the existence of the church. As a leader you must set the standard of honesty and integrity; deal with lies in the church as they arise, stop them at source and then the church will grow in truth rather than degenerate into a nest of infighting and destruction. That's what the enemy desires to see – the church pulled apart by deception. You, the leader, must ensure lies have no place in the local church. Set the standard for truth and integrity.

If the leader demonstrates great confidentiality in their lives, this integrity and sincerity will be noticed by others, then as a person of trust they will also inspire others to follow. Be a leader of great integrity in how you deal with other people especially with their problems; use wisdom to help people in difficulty; develop patience as some will come back time and again to talk over the same problems. However, there comes a time when you must make decisions about these issues and encourage people to face the problem and act in accordance with God's word. This course of action will to put an end to their continued confusion, doubt and fear. A leader in whom people have confidence will soon begin to see others change their attitudes and actions for their spiritual advancement.

A note of caution here, be very careful not to get yourself into a situation that could be compromising. If a member of the opposite sex wants to discuss delicate matters with you, then you may wish to refer them to another leader of the same gender, and whenever possible have one other leader present as a witness to the discussion. This is an incentive for churches to ensure there are female leaders on the leadership team, as some delicate issues are often better dealt with by a member of the same sex. This provides a source of accountability for all concerned. Also, it is good practice with issues involving other parties to have two leaders involved in the conversation as this allows for the truth to be told and not to have one person's word against another's. It is sad that we live in a society that has produced an attitude of selfishness and lack of trust, even in the church. However, the risk of scandal, gossip and down right lies is lessened when leaders work together to deal with some delicate issues.

There is nothing to be gained by making people's business public demonstrate a character of confidentiality as this will breed trust in those you counsel.

Chapter 10: Christ Centred

> For you have died, and your life is hidden with Christ in God. Col 3:3.

I have so far suggested 9 vital characteristics of the true leader: Character; Clear Vision; Commitment; Complete Servanthood; Compassion; Courage; Communication; Complementarity; Confidentiality; there is one more vital aspect to be considered – Christ-centred leadership.

Above all else, the Christian leader must be an individual whose life is centred on Christ and Christ alone! That is, they must be people who are full of the Spirit of God, worshipping, serving, loving and embodying Christ in the world. All Christians should reflect the image of Christ; however, leaders must excel in living Christ centred lives. Acts 6:3–4 gives some insight into this characteristic:

> Therefore, brothers, pick out from among you seven men of good repute, full of the Spirit and of wisdom, whom we will appoint to this duty. But we will devote ourselves to prayer and to the ministry of the word.

These men in Acts 6 set the example for all those in service as they were simply selected to administer daily food rations to the widows. No act of service or leadership is to be despised and thought to require people who are not spiritually minded. Note how their service was going to free up the apostles to dedicate their time to praying and preaching – body ministry is essential, delegation is essential, and spirituality is essential. J. Oswald Sanders writes:

> Spiritual leadership requires Spirit filled people. Other qualities are important; to be Spirit filled is indispensable.... A person can have a brilliant mind and possess artful administrative skill. But without spirituality he is incapable of giving truly spiritual leadership.[30]

Sander's words cut to the very heart of the matter; the church is a spiritual entity, Christ is the head, he is the true example for all other leaders, and he must be central to their lives and experience. If we have unspiritual and non-Christ-centred leaders, we will only produce unspiritual Christians in an ineffective church which is no more than a social club. However, spiritual Christ-centred leaders will produce congregations that are on fire for Jesus and make an impact on society. The world needs a Christ-centred spiritual church, for this is the only answer to its needs. The book of Acts illustrates how a well taught group of leaders (Acts 1:1–4) experienced the dynamic difference in their lives (1:5–8; 2:1–11) and made an impact on society (Acts 6:7). This could only be achieved by spiritual people leading Christ centred lives. Sanders continues:

---

[30] Sanders, *Spiritual Leadership*, 79.

The one called by God to spiritual leadership can be confident that the Holy Spirit has given him or her all necessary gifts for the service at hand.[31]

God never leaves the one called without the gifts to fulfil the calling. However, the individual must never take these gifts for granted and should endeavour through great spiritual discipline to nurture these gifts and graces to flourish in the things of God. As the leader grows personally in spiritual matters so too those who follow will be encouraged to press higher in the spiritual realm and know more of God in their lives. This results from a life of abiding in Christ.

Abiding in Christ is best illustrated in John 15:1–11.

What principles can you see in these verses that will help you grow in spirituality?

The life of Christ in the individual is only obtained as the individual is a part of the main vine; i.e. the Christian should always live close to Jesus allowing his presence to be ever present in their life and experience. The leader should set the example of this spiritual vitality and relationship with Jesus daily. As they do and flourish in spiritual things, there will be a desire stirred in others to want to be close to the Lord.

How is this achieved?

    I)   Prayer (1 Tim 2:1).

---

[31] Sanders, *Spiritual Leadership*, 83

II) Reading (2 Tim 4:13) (both the Bible and other theological and devotional material).

III) Fellowship (1 Cor 14:26).

IV) Correct use of time (Eph 5:16). Make sure you don't waste time on secondary matters when essential things are neglected.

V) Rest (Mark 6:30–32). Jesus is not a task master all leaders need to rest spend time alone with God (and your family, for they sacrifice much for you to do your work). An exhausted leader is of no use to the church of Jesus Christ. Learn to say 'no', recharge yourself and then get back to work.

VI) Failure (Matt 26:69–75). All true leaders must experience failure as this will drive them closer to the Lord. Peter failed in his early ministry career, and yet Acts 2:14–36 reveals a man full of faith, power and authority. Don't fear failure but use it as a spur to greater service.

What we achieve in leadership will only result from a life dedicated to Christ Beasley-Murray writes:

The prime qualification for a leader in the context of a church is to be a man or woman of God. Only so can the task be achieved, the team be built, and the needs of individuals be met. To be men or women of God, however, demands that leaders work constantly at their relationship with their Lord….

The leader's spiritual life needs to be constantly deepened. Progress needs to be made in the Christian life.[32]

Your success or failure in leadership does not depend on your personal strengths, gifts, abilities or respect in the community; it depends upon your relationship to Jesus. If you are called by God to serve in leadership, never take the task lightly but endeavour to remain a man or woman of God. He called you, and he will equip you, but only if you stay close to the Lord.

Being Christ-centred will affect who you are and how you lead. One major aspect of leadership from a biblical perspective which summarises leading a Christ-centred life is, 'leading from love'. Love must be the benchmark of all leaders, as this is the standard set by Jesus: 'love one another as I have loved you' (John 15:12). Is love the benchmark of your leadership style?

Leading with Love

Servant hood and leadership are brought together in one phrase, 'leading with love'. This is foundational to all true Christian leadership, love must be at the basis of all the leader does in their role.

1. Primarily there must be a love for God (John 21:15–17). Peter was asked if he loved Christ more than the water, boats, fish, other

---

[32] Beasley-Murray, *Dynamic*, 217–218.

disciples. Whatever Jesus spoke of it was all because Peter was being called to lead from love! Love for the Lord had to be paramount in his life in order to be an effective leader.

2. The leader must be controlled by the love of God (2 Cor 5:14). It is love that holds us together in this work and ministry of leadership. Paul here is relating his call to be an ambassador for the Lord and states it's only the love of God which kept him in this work. Love keeps us in our station and on the correct path; the true leader must be directed by the love of God.

3. The leader must love the people of God (Col 4:12–13). Leadership is hard work. Epaphras had worked hard for the benefit of Paul and the people at Colossae. Epaphroditus almost died in the cause of serving Paul on behalf of the church at Philippi (Phil 2:25-29). Only a deep-seated love for the people of God will allow leaders to suffer the hardships in order to see the people brought to a mature person in Christ.

Jesus illustrates this vital principle in his ministry (Mark 6:34, where 'compassion' means to have the bowels yearn!) Compassion is an inner deep desire to help and to feel sympathy. That's an essential starting place if you have no compassion for the people then you shouldn't be attempting to lead them.

Then notice what Jesus did for those he loved; he taught them! Why? Because he was concerned that they were wandering aimlessly through life with no true direction. The true leader does not want their people to miss out on what God has for them in their lives & this is best transmitted through teaching them the principles of the word of God.

Also note Mark 6:37–44. The leader has a natural concern for the people, as when Jesus realised their physical needs had to be met and supplied them food. Sometimes the leader must take notice of the practical issues people in their congregation face and not be too proud to do something about it!

Love is a principle that should dominate the Christian community and the leader should set the standard for loving the people. Is this a good definition of your attitude to the things and people of God; does love dictate your actions?

It is vital for a leader to live a Christ-centred life, as people will only progress as far as their leaders will take them. If your life is centred in Christ, then you will have the authority and compassion to draw people closer to the Lord. As people come closer to Jesus and become more Christ-like, then an attitude of love will pervade the church community and make your task of leadership easier. Be a Christ-centred leader, put Christ first in your life and let him make you the leader he desires and requires for his church.

Leadership can be a difficult thing at times, but a life centred on Christ will bring the rewards of a life of service and leadership that will see the people of God grow and engage in missional activity. Don't be afraid to lead but always lead with God as your guide!

Post-script: The Seriousness of Leadership Acts 20:17–38

Leadership in the local Christian community is often relegated to a 'whoever is available or willing to do it' rationale. This is a very sad reflection on the congregation, as I believe it illustrates a total disregard for the seriousness of the church leadership. One should be humble in one's response to the invitation to leadership, due to the gravity of the task entrusted to the individual. This is not just something to do because no one else will do it; it is a divine appointment carrying much responsibility, privilege and opportunity.

As a brief reflection on this whole subject I would like to turn to Acts 20:17–38 to highlight the seriousness of leadership.

From these verses we can highlight some very important principles that the 21st century leader should be aware of and endeavour to adopt the same within their leadership paradigm. It will also challenge the prospective or current leader as to the reasons behind leadership and it may provide individuals with the opportunity to seriously consider if they should be involved in leadership. The seriousness of leadership is highlighted in a variety of ways in these few verses.

1. *The Source of Leadership* is highlighted and illustrates the calling to leadership and the resultant responsibilities.

V.19 – leadership centres on the Lord, the one supreme in authority, the controller, God the Lord and master. Christian leadership is not about the individual – it is about God; the Lord must be at the centre. It is his church and the leaders are guardians of the people of God.

V.21 continues the theme through the necessity of one presenting 'repentance' toward God and the Lord Jesus Christ; again, the leader is not central. It all focusses on God. The central message of the church must revolve around repentance and salvation; a leader must first be a disciple who calls others to the cross.

V.24 reminds the Ephesian elders that Paul and they had received their ministry from the Lord himself. All who are called to leadership are so called because it is the Lord's desire that they be given the task. Therefore, it is essential that people do not simply accept a leadership position if they are not convinced it is God's will. People should show aptitude for the task, skills, gifts, humility and willingness but they must be God's choice and not man's decision.

V.25 Paul reminds his listeners that all their preaching must centre on the kingdom of God, not on Paul or themselves, but on a future spiritual kingdom of which we already have a foretaste. The spiritual nature of leadership cannot be over-emphasised; we are dealing with a spiritual kingdom, spiritual principles, and spiritual life and death.

V.26 Paul relates the seriousness of leading and proclaiming the gospel, he relates how he could not be held to account for those who chose to reject the message. He will not be held accountable for them as the issue of salvation is between God and the individual. The true leader is called to dispense the message and leave the rest to God. However, it is a matter of life and death.

V.28 offers a further reminder that we have received our ministry and calling through the work of the Holy Spirit. Here we see the Trinity represented in one's call to service. The Father, Son and Spirit all play a role in bringing the individual to a place of fitness for leadership. If we ignore the call of God or try to produce a call that is not there, then spiritual disaster is likely to ensue for both individual and congregation.

The seriousness of leadership is realised in the fact that it is of and from God and is not of human origin. That is why leaders must be spiritually minded in order not to become conceited and dictatorial; and why congregations should respect the leaders as they are given by God to serve the people. Leaders are directly accountable to the local church but ultimately accountable to God who called them to serve.

The Sensitivity of Leadership. Another aspect of true leadership is the sensitivity of leadership. Sadly, too many leaders in local congregations can suffer from 'foot in mouth' disease and can be totally insensitive as they deal with people. People have problems, troubles, difficulties, worries, concerns and doubts; the leader must be sensitive to these issues and know how to respond to everyone in a manner befitting the God whom they serve and the situation that confronts the people. Love, compassion, concern and a helping spirit are vital in he leader.

V.19 introduces a word which many 21st century Christians dislike; humility! In respect to leadership, I believe this means one must be aware of one's own weakness and inabilities; who is sufficient for the task of leading God's people? The leader must not be arrogant and self-promoting. When one is aware of personal weakness it is much easier to deal with the problems of others. Why? Because there is a deeper understanding or realisation of the human mind and a greater empathy with people who are the same as the leader. If the leader cannot understand themselves how will they ever understand others and how will help ever be offered to them to restore or revive?

Care for the flock arises from one's understanding and application of the word of God (vv. 20, 27). The leader must be a biblically literate individual for the 'flock' or local church will only be helped by the impartation of the word of God into the lives of individuals. Congregations need the word of God in its entirety both the hard bits and the nice bits (2 Pet.3:16). Beware leaders who only ever deal with the well-known, well-worn passages of encouragement on love, grace, and mercy and avoid some of the difficult areas of holiness, devotion, dedication, sacrifice, tithing and the like. All church members require a balanced diet and some things can be hard to digest but they do serve a vital purpose in strengthening the church. V.28 'feed' is derived from the root word poimen "to shepherd" which means to tend, care, feed and rule. Leadership has a wide-ranging impact upon the congregation; this will be more acceptable and beneficial if it emanates from the 'whole counsel of God' or the complete word of God. Seriousness of handling the word of God is required; some questions to consider:

i) What is your view of the Bible?
ii) How familiar are you with the biblical narrative, content and theology?
iii) Do you depend on the word of God for guidance and help?
iv) Do you desire others to accept and apply the word of God?

A sincere heart is expressed in vv.19, 31 tears shed on behalf of the local Christian community. A true leader will be a person who has a heart for the people and is not afraid or ashamed to shed tears in God's presence for those people. Jesus cried so why shouldn't we? There are depths of sorrow, heart ache and concern for people's well-being that will on occasions reduce the leader to tears; don't be afraid to cry! However, be sure to take the grief to the Lord.

Further sensitivity is noted in the fact that Paul warns the leaders to watch out for false teachers as he does not want anyone to suffer spiritually due to false ministry (vv. 29–31). A leader must be sensitive to the situations that people find themselves in especially in respect to what they are listening to from the pulpit. I suggest that the greatest area of importance for the leader is to ensure the truth is preached and when error is detected it is dealt with quickly and efficiently. Know the word, know the doctrine, stand for the truth and protect the people.

The Sacrifice of Leadership. The final area is that of the sacrifice of leadership; again, an area that many modern-day Christian leaders are not happy to entertain. Why should I sacrifice anything for the people at church? The main reason behind the issue of sacrifice is the example of the Lord Jesus (Phil 2:1–8). The sacrificial attitude of the Lord is something disciples should seek to emulate, and leaders should be setting the example.

V.19 refers to plots and schemes of the Jews – opposition is a key element of leadership; Paul faced many trials and persecution is always a possibility especially for leaders. This persecution can take many forms often depending upon one's cultural setting. The opposition can range from gossip about a leader's life style from within the fellowship to imprisonment and death.

Uncertainty of the future is another sacrifice, leaders often face (v. 22). Most people plan their lives around their specific desires and abilities to achieve things. Paul here identifies sacrificing one's future to God's leading – who knows what may be in store for the truly dedicated leader. When one truly accepts the role of Christian leadership it is essential to be open to the direction of God which can sometimes run contrary to personal preference.

Life is even to be sacrificed if necessary (v.24). Life is not to be despised, but it must not be clung on to as if it were the most precious thing possessed. If the leader or Christian is called to give their life it is the greatest sacrifice for the cause of the gospel. This follows the ultimate example of the Lord Jesus.

V.32 the goal of leadership is the spiritual growth and maturity of others; all the leader does they do for the benefit of others. It can be difficult for us in a very self-centred cultural setting to put others first sometimes to personal detriment; however self-sacrificing character is a key feature of the true leader.

The sacrifice of financial reward or even stability is another major area of concern for the leader. Verses 33–35 describe a picture of an individual who was free from covetousness, the leader should not be a 'money grabber' or jealous of another's success. They should not be afraid to work in secular employment to support their ministry (v. 34). Hard work is commendable, and the Christian should be the best employee in the company always working hard to please his employer and achieve success in work (v. 35).

Sacrifice is further noted as resulting in helping others who are 'weak'. This could be physically weak and unable to work; is Paul intimating here that he supported such people? Or it could refer to those who are spiritually weak in faith of which there will be many in your life as a leader. The leader must never despise the weak but endeavour to encourage and support; this will require sacrifice of time, finance, strength and family however the true leader is a giver not a taker! Giving is at the very heart of God and hence Christian leaders are called to mirror that divine characteristic. The one who gave all, sacrificed all has called us to do the same.

Are you aware of the seriousness of leadership? If you feel called to leadership in the local Christian community it is imperative that you are made aware of the seriousness of leadership. If these issues are too much and you feel it is inappropriate for you to be involved in this kind of leadership then you must take stock of your calling and desires. I would further suggest that you speak to the pastor or mentor and discuss further how you feel about the seriousness of leadership as you plan to move forward in your Christian ministry.

It is a very serious thing to be involved in church leadership however, there is no greater work in which to be involved.